Happy Birthday
Johnathan

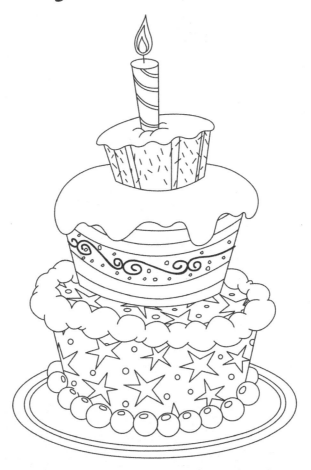

The BIG Birthday
Activity Book

BirthdayDr

CONTENTS

Happy Birthday Johnathan; I hope you enjoy this book. It is jam packed with cool stuff for you to do from crosswords, word searches, drawing and coloring.

It has loads of fun things for you to do on your big day.

Have FUN – Happy Birthday Johnathan

FOR YOUR PARENTS

Thank you for buying this book, it will keep Johnathan engaged and will help improve writing and math skills

It is also a good break from TV and computer games

Keep it safe as it is a great keepsake of your child's early years

If you and Johnathan like this book please leave us a review

We have lots of other personalized books to check out at:

www.BirthdayDr.com

Including:

Happy Halloween Johnathan – Spooky Activity Book

Merry Christmas Johnathan – Activity Book

Happy Easter Johnathan – Activity Book

And many more …

Happy
Birthday
Johnathan

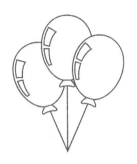

Your Name: **Johnathan** _____

Age: _____

What you did on your birthday:

_____

_____

Where you went on your birthday:

_____

Presents you got for your birthday:

_____

Johnathan, did you know…

When your age and your date of birth are the same, it is a special day known as your Golden Birthday

So if you were born on the 10th of the month, your 10th birthday would be your golden birthday

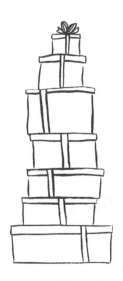

Birthday Jokes

Birthday Jokes

What did the grumpy birthday candle say at the party?
Birthdays burn me up

When would you hit a birthday cake with a hammer?
When it's a pound cake

Where do you find birthday presents for cats?
In a cat-alogue

What do George Washington, Christopher Columbus and Abraham Lincoln all have in common?
They were all born on holidays!

How do you celebrate Moby Dick's birthday?
With a whale of a party!

Why do we put candles on top of a birthday cake?
Because it's too hard to put them on the bottom

What goes up and never comes down?
Your age

Why did the boy put the cake in the freezer?
Because he wanted to ice it

What song did they sing to the dancer on her birthday?
Tappy birthday to you

What did the turtle do on his birthday?
He shell-abrated

Why did the birthday cake go to see the doctor?
Because it was feeling crumby

What has a long tail, wings and wears a colorful bow?
A birthday pheasant

Why did the boy get soap for his birthday?
It was a soap-rize party

Which birthday party game do rabbits like the most?
Musical hares

Why was the birthday cake so hard?
It was a marble cake

Why couldn't cavemen send birthday cards?
The stamps kept falling off the rocks

When is a birthday cake like a golf ball?
When it's sliced

Did you hear about the pine tree's birthday?
It was really sappy

Why did the baby put candles on the toilet?
He wanted to have a birthday potty

Why are birthday's good for you?
People who have the most live the longest

What did the birthday balloon say to the pin?
"Hi, Buster"

What do you give a nine-hundred-pound gorilla for his birthday?
I don't know, but you'd better hope he likes it

"Doctor, I get heartburn every time I eat birthday cake"
"Next time, take off the candles"

Did you hear about the flag's birthday?
It was a Flappy one

Why won't anyone eat the dogs birthday cake?
Because he always slobbers out the candles

What did the ice cream say to the unhappy cake?
"Hey, what's eating you?"

What are your two favourite times to party?
Daytime and night-time

What do they serve at birthday parties in heaven?
Angel food cake, of course

What is an elf's favourite kind of birthday cake?
Shortcake

What does a cat like to eat on his birthday?
Mice cream and cake

Knock, knock!
Who's there?
Jimmy
Jimmy who?
Jimmy some ice cream and cake! I'm hungry

What usually comes after the monster lights the birthday candles?
The fire department

What does the hungry monster get after he's eaten too much ice cream?
More ice cream

What did the big candle say to the little candle?
"You're too young to go out"

Why did the boy feel warm on his birthday?
Because people kept toasting him

Cat: "What did you get him for his birthday?"
Dog: "Pant . . . pant!"
Cat: "Great . . . he needs a pair of pants"

Knock, knock!
Who's there?
Mark
Mark who?
Mark your calendars, my birthday's next month

What do you always get on your birthday?
Another year older

Why did you buy me a pair of bunny ears?
I wanted you to have a hoppy birthday

What does a basketball player do before he blows out his candles?
He makes a swish

Why was the monster standing on his head at the birthday party?
He heard they were having upside-down cake

Knock, knock!
Who's there?
Wanda
Wanda who?
Wanda wish you a happy birthday

Birthday Activities for Johnathan

Word search, crossword and other fun activities

Answers are on the back of each puzzle page ... no peeking

Big Birthday Word Search

Happy   Birthday   Johnathan

Party   Cake   Candles

Songs   Presents   Balloons

F	L	T	S	E	L	D	N	A	C	C	T
B	A	L	L	O	O	N	S	C	Q	O	N
P	I	K	F	U	L	E	K	A	C	Y	A
A	K	I	K	P	I	Y	Q	W	A	L	H
F	F	D	Y	P	P	A	H	D	M	P	T
S	L	O	B	Q	U	K	H	K	R	S	A
L	A	Y	M	Q	V	T	A	E	U	V	N
X	U	T	B	X	R	A	S	O	J	J	H
U	S	R	E	I	O	E	N	Z	C	C	O
G	H	A	B	K	N	F	B	Z	U	V	J
U	R	P	R	T	F	B	D	Q	T	Q	S
V	Q	V	S	O	N	G	S	D	O	F	W

Big Birthday Word Search Answers

Happy	Birthday	Johnathan
Party	Cake	Candles
Songs	Presents	Balloons

Big Birthday Crossword

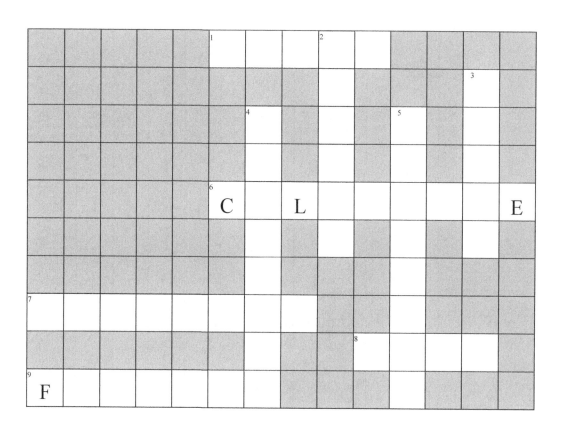

Across

1. You should get these in the mail
6. Let's C _ L _____ E your birthday
7. They go pop at parties
8. Candles go on it
9. They will come to your Party
   (Hint: begins with F)

Down

2. You pin the tail on this during parties
3. Let's take a selfie
4. You will get lots of these today
5. Happy _____ to you

Big Birthday Crossword Answers

						C	A	R	D	S			
								O					P
						P		N		B		H	
						R		K		I		O	
					C	E	L	E	B	R	A	T	E
						S		Y		T		O	
						E				H			
B	A	L	L	O	O	N	S			D			
						T		C	A	K	E		
F	R	I	E	N	D	S				Y			

Across

1. You should get these in the mail
6. Let's C _L_____E your birthday
7. They go pop at parties
8. Candles go on it
9. They will come to your Party
   (Hint: begins with F)

Down

2. You pin the tail on this during parties
3. Let's take a selfie
4. You will get lots of these today
5. Happy _____ to you

Link Up Birthday

Link the letters, to make a word or phrase

BIRTH	RDS
CA	DAY
CAN	SENT
PA	ATHAN
JOHN	RATIONS
BAN	BRATE
PRE	PRISE
DECO	DLES
CELE	NER
SUR	RTY

Link Up Birthday Answers

Link the letters, to make a word or phrase

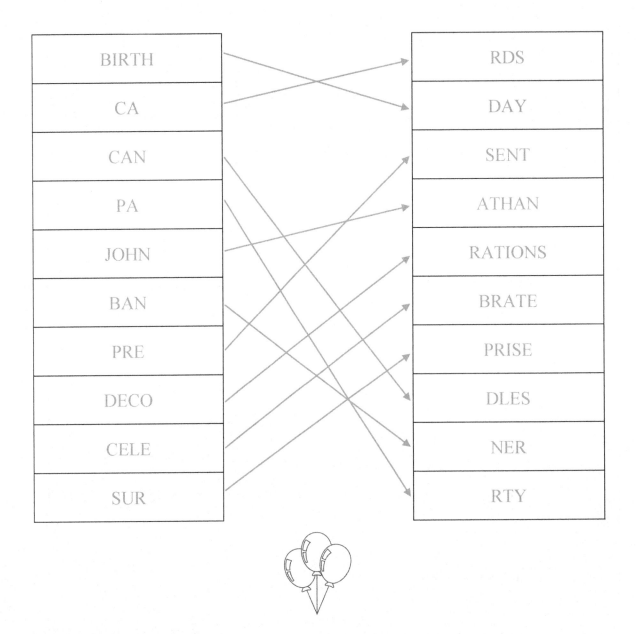

BIRTH	RDS
CA	DAY
CAN	SENT
PA	ATHAN
JOHN	RATIONS
BAN	BRATE
PRE	PRISE
DECO	DLES
CELE	NER
SUR	RTY

Party Code

Use the number codes to find the secret words

Tip (1=A, 2=B, 3=C) See last page to help, full list from A to Z

18	9	2	2	15	14

3	21	16	3	1	11	5	19

2	9	18	20	8	4	1	25

2	1	12	12	15	15	14	19

10	15	8	14	1	20	8	1	14

16	18	5	19	5	14	20	19

Party Code Answers

Use the number codes to find the secret words (Tip 1=A, 2=B, 3=C)

R	I	B	B	O	N

C	U	P	C	A	K	E	S

B	I	R	T	H	D	A	Y

B	A	L	L	O	O	N	S

J	O	H	N	A	T	H	A	N

P	R	E	S	E	N	T	S

Pinata Tile Mash Up

Rearrange the tiles to reveal the answer, write it below each one

Clue: Happy _____

| Y | RT | HD | BI | A |

_____

Clue: You hit it with a stick at Birthday parties

| TA | N | PI | A |

_____

Clue: Your presents are covered in it, before you open them

| NG_ | PPI | WRA | PER | PA |

_____

Clue: It is cold, and you often eat it at parties

| EA | E_ | IC | CR | M |

_____

Pinata Tile Mash Up Answers

Rearrange the tiles to reveal the answer

Clue: Happy _____

| Y | RT | HD | BI | A |

HAPPY BIRTHDAY

Clue: You hit it with a stick at Birthday parties

| TA | N | PI | A |

PINATA

Clue: Your presents are covered in it, before you open them

| NG_ | PPI | WRA | PER | PA |

WRAPPING PAPER

Clue: It is cold, and you often eat it at parties

| EA | E_ | IC | CR | M |

ICE CREAM

The Fallen Message Puzzle

Each letter is in the correct column, but below where it should be.

Put the letters back in the grid to rebuild the secret message

		H	P		Y		
		R	T		D	A	

		R	A	A	D	H		
J	O	H	N	H	T	Y	A	
B	I	H	T	P	P	A	Y	N

29

The Fallen Message Puzzle Answer

Each letter is in the correct column, but below where it should be.
Put the letters back in the grid to rebuild the secret message

		H	A	P	P	Y		
B	I	R	T	H	D	A	Y	
J	O	H	N	A	T	H	A	N

		R	A	A	D	H		
J	O	H	N	H	T	Y	A	
B	I	H	T	P	P	A	Y	N

Code Cracker

1. Solve the numbers puzzle

2. Convert the answer to a letter (1=A, 2=B, 3=C)
   Crack the secret code word

				Number		Letter
22	-	20	=		=	
3	+	6	=		=	
11	+	7	=		=	
6	+	14	=		=	
12	-	4	=		=	
16	-	12	=		=	
7	-	6	=		=	
13	+	12	=		=	
29	-	10	=		=	

Code Cracker Answers

1. Solve the numbers puzzle

2. Convert the answer to a letter (1=A, 2=B, 3=C)

    Crack the secret code word

Equation				Number		Letter
22	-	20	=	2	=	B
3	+	6	=	9	=	I
11	+	7	=	18	=	R
6	+	14	=	20	=	T
12	-	4	=	8	=	H
16	-	12	=	4	=	D
7	-	6	=	1	=	A
13	+	12	=	25	=	Y
29	-	10	=	19	=	S

Number Chains

1. Work out the math puzzle for each column below
2. Find the secret word, using the code (1=A, 2=B, 3=C)

16	11	18	5	14	8	12	20	17
+	+	-	+	-	+	-	+	-
3	3	8	14	12	8	6	4	2
=	=	=	=	=	=	=	=	=
+	-	+	-	+	-	+	-	+
11	13	12	10	5	6	11	8	10
=	=	=	=	=	=	=	=	=
-	+	-	-	-	+	-	+	-
27	4	10	4	5	8	16	4	20
=	=	=	=	=	=	=	=	=

Enter the letters above using the number code (1=A, 2=B, 3=C)

Number Chains Answers

1. Work out the math puzzle for each column below
2. Find the secret word, using the code (1=A, 2=B, 3=C)

16	11	18	5	14	8	12	20	17
+	+	-	+	-	+	-	+	-
3	3	8	14	12	8	6	4	2
=	=	=	=	=	=	=	=	=
19	14	10	19	2	16	6	24	15
+	-	+	-	+	-	+	-	+
11	13	12	10	5	6	11	8	10
=	=	=	=	=	=	=	=	=
30	1	22	9	7	10	17	16	25
-	+	-	-	-	+	-	+	-
27	4	10	4	5	8	16	4	20
=	=	=	=	=	=	=	=	=
3	5	12	5	2	18	1	20	5

C	E	L	E	B	R	A	T	E

Enter the letters above using the number code (1=A, 2=B, 3=C)

Well done Johnathan
Good job with the puzzles

Happy Birthday to you!
Happy Birthday to you!

Happy Birthday dear Johnathan

Happy Birthday to you

Do you want some more puzzles? And some drawing and coloring?

Coming up …

Ice Cream Mix Up

Unscramble each of the anagram clue words; we will give you a clue with the two letters

Copy the letters in the numbered blocks to reveal the hidden word

YADHTRIB

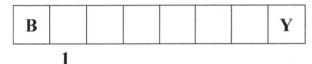

B						Y

1

LESCAND

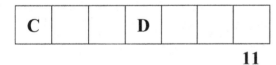

C		D			

11

PATYR

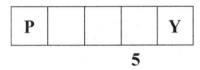

P			Y

5

BLANOOLS

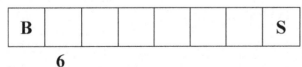

B						S

6

IFGTS

G				S

4   7

ATCVIITIES

A		T						

3   8

SGSNO

S		G	

9

NNERBA

B				R

2   10

Hidden Message

1   2   3   4   5   6   7   8   9   10   11

(Answers on the next page)

Ice Cream Mix Up Answers

Unscramble each of the anagram clue words; we will give you a clue with the first and last letters

Copy the letters in the numbered blocks to reveal the hidden word

YADHTRIB (Example)

B	I	R	T	H	D	A	Y

1

LESCAND

C	A	N	D	L	E	S

11

PATYR

P	A	R	T	Y

5

BLANOOLS

B	A	L	L	O	O	N	S

6

IFGTS

G	I	F	T	S

  4   7

ATCVHTIES

A	C	T	I	V	I	T	I	E	S

        3   8

SGSNO

S	O	N	G	S

  9

NNERBA

B	A	N	N	E	R

     2   10

Hidden Message

I	N	V	I	T	A	T	I	O	N	S
1	2	3	4	5	6	7	8	9	10	11

Birthday Maze

Can you find your way through the maze to get the birthday cake?

Word Search Party

Family   Friends   Play

Dance   Games   Ribbons

Pinata   Surprise   Chocolate

G	A	M	E	S	Q	L	J	Y	R	G	J
W	X	U	X	E	O	R	L	O	P	L	C
H	C	T	P	I	N	A	T	A	W	X	C
Y	M	U	R	I	B	B	O	N	S	H	U
X	E	Z	X	C	D	S	P	J	O	U	X
K	S	W	Y	E	D	L	O	C	Y	C	U
K	I	S	R	N	A	B	O	P	L	M	T
D	R	H	E	Y	O	L	S	N	I	H	M
X	P	I	Z	C	A	H	Z	P	M	V	F
A	R	M	G	T	P	M	P	L	A	O	S
F	U	B	E	A	N	V	K	S	F	R	A
I	S	S	V	E	C	N	A	D	T	H	O

Word Search Party Answers

Family	Friends	Play
Dance	Games	Ribbons
Pinata	Surprise	Chocolate

G	A	M	E	S	Q	L	J	Y	R	G	J
W	X	U	X	E	O	R	L	O	P	L	C
H	C	T	P	I	N	A	T	A	W	X	C
Y	M	U	R	I	B	B	O	N	S	H	U
X	E	Z	X	C	D	S	P	J	O	U	X
K	S	W	Y	E	D	L	O	C	Y	C	U
K	I	S	R	N	A	B	O	P	L	M	T
D	R	H	E	Y	O	L	S	N	I	H	M
X	P	I	Z	C	A	H	Z	P	M	V	F
A	R	M	G	T	P	M	P	L	A	O	S
F	U	B	E	A	N	V	K	S	F	R	A
I	S	S	V	E	C	N	A	D	T	H	O

Code Cakes

Use the number codes to find the secret words

Tip (1=A, 2=B, 3=C) Look at the back page to help, full list from A to Z

4	15

25	15	21

23	1	14	20

19	15	13	5

2	9	18	20	8	4	1	25

3	1	11	5

Code Cakes Answers

Use the number codes to find the secret words

Tip (1=A, 2=B, 3=C) Look at the back page to help, full list from A to Z

4	15
D	O

25	15	21
Y	O	U

23	1	14	20
W	A	N	T

19	15	13	5
S	O	M	E

2	9	18	20	8	4	1	25
B	I	R	T	H	D	A	Y

3	1	11	5
C	A	K	E

Candle Cracker

1. Solve the numbers puzzle

2. Convert the answer to a letter (1=A, 2=B, 3=C).
   Crack the secret code word

				Number		Letter
7	-	4	=		=	
2	+	3	=		=	
18	-	6	=		=	
9	-	4	=		=	
14	-	12	=		=	
9	+	9	=		=	
19	-	18	=		=	
6	+	14	=		=	
17	-	12	=		=	

47

Candle Cracker Answers

1. Solve the numbers puzzle

2. Convert the answer to a letter (1=A, 2=B, 3=C).
   Crack the secret code word

				Number		Letter
7	-	4	=	3	=	C
2	+	3	=	5	=	E
18	-	6	=	12	=	L
9	-	4	=	5	=	E
14	-	12	=	2	=	B
9	+	9	=	18	=	R
19	-	18	=	1	=	A
6	+	14	=	20	=	T
17	-	12	=	5	=	E

Party Popper

1. Work out the math puzzle for each column below
2. Find the secret word, using the code (1=A, 2=B, 3=C)

12	19	6	9	18	15	20	6	7
+	-	-	+	-	+	-	+	-
6	16	2	9	12	5	6	4	2
=	=	=	=	=	=	=	=	=
+	+	+	-	+	-	+	-	+
11	3	12	8	5	12	4	8	8
=	=	=	=	=	=	=	=	=
-	+	-	-	+	+	-	+	-
26	2	1	7	4	4	17	18	8
=	=	=	=	=	=	=	=	=

☐ ☐ ☐ ☐ ☐ ☐ ☐ ☐ ☐

Enter the letters above using the number code (1=A, 2=B, 3=C)

Party Popper Answers

1. Work out the math puzzle for each column below
2. Find the secret word, using the code (1=A, 2=B, 3=C)

12	19	6	9	18	15	20	6	7
+	-	-	+	-	+	-	+	-
6	16	2	9	12	5	6	4	2
=	=	=	=	=	=	=	=	=
18	**3**	**4**	**18**	**6**	**20**	**14**	**10**	**5**
+	+	+	-	+	-	+	-	+
11	3	12	8	5	12	4	8	8
=	=	=	=	=	=	=	=	=
29	**6**	**16**	**10**	**11**	**8**	**18**	**2**	**13**
-	+	-	-	+	+	-	+	-
26	2	1	7	4	4	17	18	8
=	=	=	=	=	=	=	=	=
3	8	15	3	15	12	1	20	5

C	H	O	C	O	L	A	T	E

Enter the letters above using the number code (1=A, 2=B, 3=C)

Birthday Brains

Name: Johnathan

How many words to do with birthdays can you make

Complete against a friend

Whoever has the most words will win

Tear these two pages out, so you can both complete it at the same time

Cake	Birthday	Banner

Birthday Brains

Name: _____

How many words to do with birthdays can you make

Complete against a friend

Whoever has the most words will win

Tear these two pages out, so you can both complete it at the same time

Cake	Birthday	Banner

Decorate the Cake

Color the Ice Creams

Color the Presents

Draw your favorite Present Johnathan

My present is: _____

We hope you enjoy your Birthday Johnathan

Don't forget to thank your Parents

On the next page you can write them a letter, fill in the blanks, tear it out carefully and surprise them

Dear _____

Thank you so much for a great birthday, I had a great time at

_____

Thank you for all my amazing presents, some of my favorite presents are

_____

_____

_____

Love

_____

Johnathan   xxx

Decorate your own Happy Birthday Banner

| H | A | P | P | Y | 🎈 | B | I | R | T | H | D | A | Y |

| J | O | H | N | A | T | H | A | N |

Instructions:

1. Color each letter on each page

2. Cut each page out carefully

3. Stick them together side by side

The final sign will say

| H | A | P | P | Y | 🎈 | B | I | R | T | H | D | A | Y |

| J | O | H | N | A | T | H | A | N |

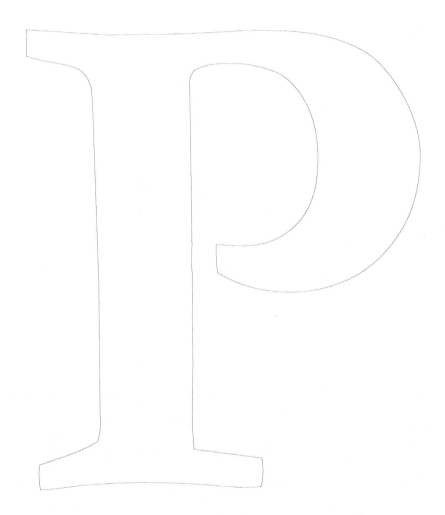

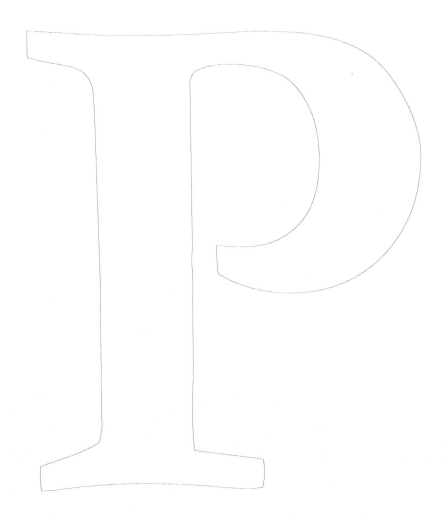

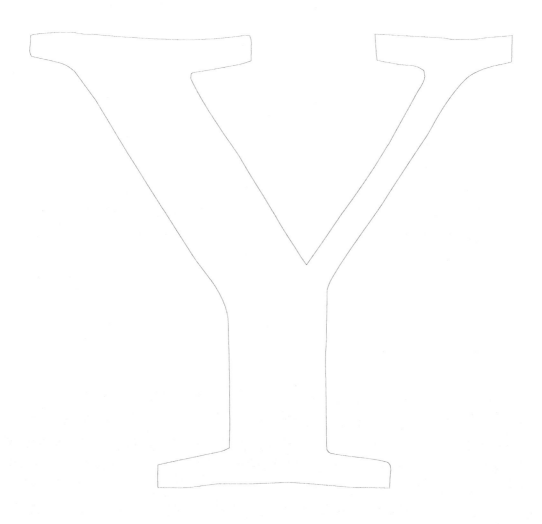

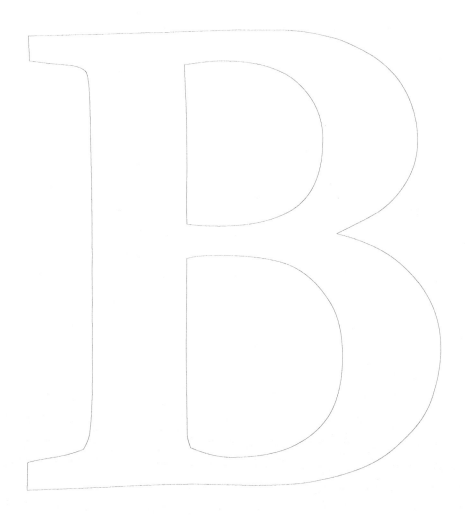

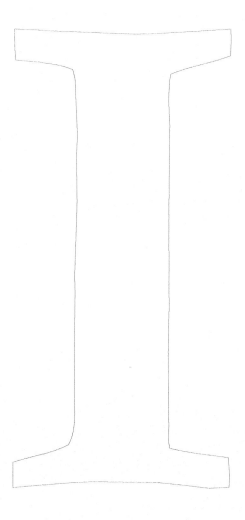

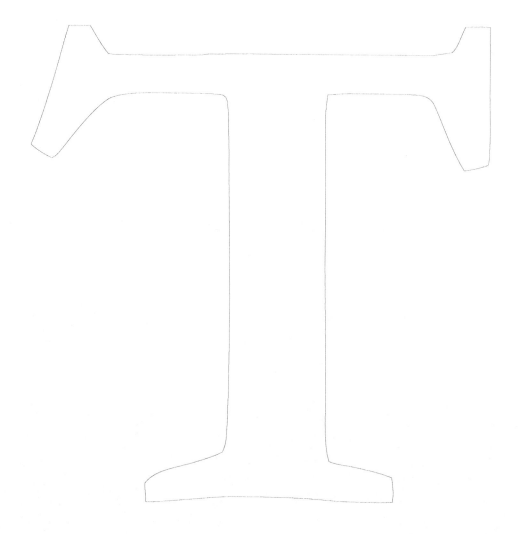

95

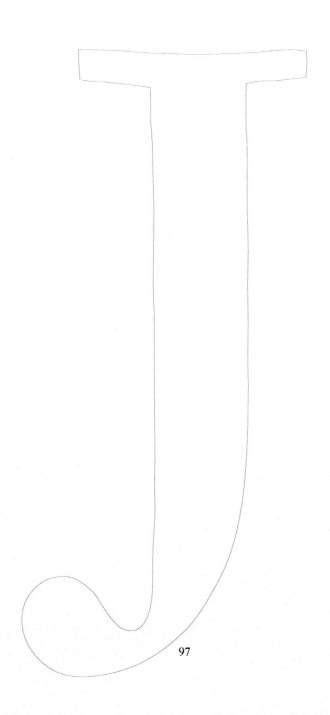

97

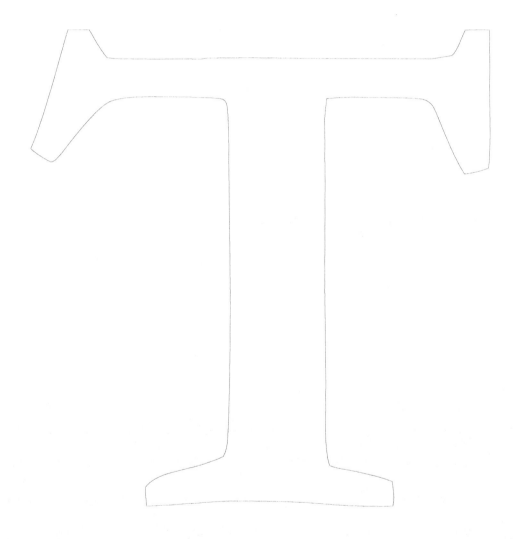

Have a great
Birthday

JOHNATHAN

If you liked this book please leave us a review

We have lots of other personalized books to check out at:

www.BirthdayDr.com

Including:

Happy Halloween Johnathan – Spooky Activity Book

Merry Christmas Johnathan – Activity Book

Happy Easter Johnathan – Activity Book

And many more …

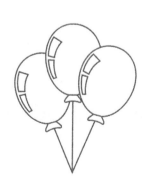  

Number Codes

1 = A
2 = B
3 = C
4 = D
5 = E
6 = F
7 = G
8 = H
9 = I
10 = J
11 = K
12 = L
13 = M
14 = N
15 = O
16 =P
17 = Q
18 = R
19 = S
20 = T
21 = U
22 = V
23 = W
24 = X
25 = Y
26 = Z

Made in the USA
Middletown, DE
06 June 2022

66743384R00066